Pinterest for Business: a Complete, Updated Guide for Ultimate Success

Christine Corretti, Ph.D.

Table of Contents

Introduction

This book is different from others about Pinterest. It provides detailed, methodical, instructions on how to use and optimize Pinterest, with all its updates, for business. Here you will find a great deal of insight into why and how brands have gathered such a large following and sales from having a presence on what is the fastest growing social media platform of its time. This book will save you money, time, frustration and worry by disclosing secrets to gaining visibility within and sales from the Pinterest community. What I have written here is the product of extensive research and reading on the subject, as well as first-hand experience using Pinterest for business and pleasure. I have studied all available literature on the topic and have even spoken to top social media specialists about my project. The resulting book assimilates, assesses and adds tremendously to current knowledge of Pinterest's importance to businesses. In short, this text, which covers basic to advanced techniques, is all you need to flourish as a business by using Pinterest.

The book unfolds in the following manner. A brief history of Pinterest precedes an explanation of how this social media site operates technically and aesthetically and why it has become so popular. Chapter 1 also discusses who Pinterest appeals to and why, points that are absolutely necessary to understanding the marketing power of Pinterest.

Chapter 2 gives you something you will not find in another book: a fully explained, step-by-step guide to easily and quickly converting your Pinterest Profile (a.k.a. personal) Page into a Business Page. You will learn about the similarities and differences between a Profile Page and a Business Page and how the latter will benefit your Pinterest presence and sales. In addition, I provide insider information, including the <u>right</u> way to make hashtags effective, on how to tailor your Business Page for Search Engine Optimization (SEO). Chapter 2 also offers an art historian's/artist's instruction and insight on how to make your Business Page stand out and shine in the imagistic ocean that is Pinterest.

Chapter 3 details how to design your profile for a successful media marketing plan, attract and KEEP followers. As you will learn, the right methods of engagement will increase your sales tremendously.

The fourth chapter discusses strategies that big and small businesses have employed to maximize their earnings through Pinterest.

Chapter 5 outlines how to link your Pinterest Page to Facebook, Twitter, and email accounts. I disclose new and lesser known ways of spreading your Pinfluence across cyberspace.

The last section discusses Pinterest's future in the online world and what that could mean for your marketing plans. Instruction given here will enable you to rise in what I foresee as the next phase of internet marketing.

Chapter 1 Pinterest Defined: Use and Value

Pinterest was founded by Paul Sciarra, Evan Sharp and Ben Silberman, who launched the social media platform in March, 2010. Since then Pinterest has been growing at an immense speed, although it still lags behind such giants as Facebook and Twitter in audience reach. Pinterest is the fastest growing social media network of its time. In December, 2010 Pinterest was already number 7 in the top 10 social media sites, ahead of Google+ and Tumblr and behind Facebook, LinkedIn, Twitter, Tagged, MySpace, and myYearbook. It jumped from 9 million users in December, 2011 to 48 million just twelve months later. On average Pinterest currently has over 4 million daily users. In March, 2012 alone Pinterest had 23 billion page views. With such an enormous audience it is no wonder that Pinterest is now searching for new ways to capitalize on its success. The company has expanded its funding to $200 million, which raises its current valuation to $2.5 billion.[1]

How to use Pinterest: Overview

Pinterest's quick and easy mode of operation is partly responsible for its popularity. An online pin board, Pinterest allows users to "pin" images (videos and notes included) that interest them; hence the combination of the terms "pin" and "interest." Viewers can collect, organize, showcase, and share images from the web by pinning (via the "Pin it" button on websites) and repining them onto their own theme-based boards (or, if invited, onto others' boards), and "liking" images (which then go into the user's "likes" file at the top of his/her main board page).

To get started, create a Pinterest Profile or, as the next chapter will discuss, a Business Page. One can sign up for and in to Pinterest with one's Twitter account, or a personal (not fan/business) Facebook account. Both can be unlinked from Pinterest at any time.

After the computer walks you through the various steps of creating a Page (entering your name, photo, password, etc.), which you can later edit by clicking the small pencil on your ID box, you will be asked to follow a few boards before you can start your own (figure 1). Follow boards with themes that interest you. If you're a fashionista, for example, you

Figure 1 Profile box featuring editing pencil at far right.

may choose boards on Paris runway shows and top fashion designers. You have the choice to follow one, a few, or all of a pinner's boards. Your decision is important because whenever followers pin new images to their boards those pictures will come into your image feed, which you can access in the categories menu that appears when you hover over the striated box at the top of your Page, or simply by clicking the red word "Pinterest" at the top/center of your screen. That feed will inspire you and you'll begin collecting and sharing new pins in no time. All you have to do is hover your cursor over a pin and the options "pin," (to avoid confusion, I will often use the term "repin" here), onto one of your own boards, and "like" will appear (figure 2). At this point you do not need to worry about citing pins' sources, as all pins are linked back to their original venues via captioned urls and their pinners' names.

You can always "unfollow" boards later and the images from those boards will no longer appear in your feed, but it is

Figure 2 Enlarged pin with buttons at top.

a good idea to follow at least a dozen or so in order to get the most out of the Pinterest experience (n.b. when you "unfollow" someone Pinterest will not notify that person that you've done so). Plus, as the next chapter will discuss at length, whenever you follow a person it is HIGHLY likely that he/she will follow *you*. The number of one's followers and of those one is following is found at the top-right of one's boards display.

As you find followers you will notice that, many Pinterest users are female. In America alone 80% of those who use the site are women. Most boards on the two most popular topics on Pinterest – fashion and crafts – belong to women. Other subjects on Pinterest that are by/for women include cosmetics, skin care, jewelry, architecture and interior design.

A good number of those who use Pinterest are on the site to get ideas for what to buy (70%), to collect things that interest them (67%), and to follow the latest trends (67%). (Bizrate Insight survey August, 2012). Bizrate's Insight survey of August, 2012 shows that 69% of Pinterest users found an item on the site that they purchased or wanted to buy. (Purchases can be made through pins' urls and the "website" box on enlarged pins that lead directly to second and third party shopping venues; see figure 2.) Pinterest incites and caters to viewers' buying intent not only through its myriad of images, but also through featured comments on product values, which clearly enhance product referrals.

Pinterest is therefore a marketer's dream: pins have great potential to go viral and attract millions of buyers from all over the world. No wonder more and more businesses are tapping into the money-making power of Pinterest. The next chapter will explain the first step in doing the same.

Chapter 2 Your Pinterest Business Page: Why You Need it and What You Must Make of It

It is now mandatory for anyone who uses Pinterest for business purposes to convert his/her Profile (personal) Page into a Business Page. The process can be tricky, but this is book will simplify the process and show you how to maximize the benefits of having a business account with Pinterest.

Join, or Convert

When you first arrive at Pinterest's homepage, you will see two buttons. One of them, in red, says "JOIN PINTEREST." The other is an option to login if you already have an account. When you click "JOIN PINTEREST" you will have a new screen in front of you. At the bottom of that screen is an option to "learn more" if you are a business. Click on "learn more" and you will see a new page (business.pinterest.com) that says "Millions of people use Pinterest to discover and share things that inspire them." At the bottom of that message is the command "Join as a Business." The same page has a box that says "Get Started." Clicking on either "Join as a Business" or "Get Started" will lead you to the next steps to create a business Page.

If you already have a Pinterest account you can just hover over the striated menu box at the top of your Page to see the term "Businesses" at the bottom of the categories menu (figure 3). Click on that word to go to the screen where you can convert your account to a Business Page.

<u>Figure 3</u> <u>Categories displayed by hovering over the striated</u> <u>menu box at the top left corner of your Pinterest Page.</u>

In addition, the words "Get Started" just at the top of your boards leads to business.pinterest.com (see figure 1).

Note that you cannot have two Pinterest accounts (i.e. a personal one and another for business) under the same name and email address.

The process of creating a Business Page involves a number of boxes to fill, including business type (it is **very** important to specify who you are so you can show up in searches), contact name, email (use a business address), profile photo (add one of yourself or a business logo), location (so people can easily find you and you can network with others in your area), password, etc. This part of the process is self-explanatory, but keep in mind that entering a description in the "About" box with many keywords describing your business/brand will help you rise in online search results. And do not neglect adding your business website url in the "About" box. There will also be a separate box for your website address, but the more places that url appears the greater your potential to rise in online searches will be (figure 4). Read and accept the "Terms of Service."

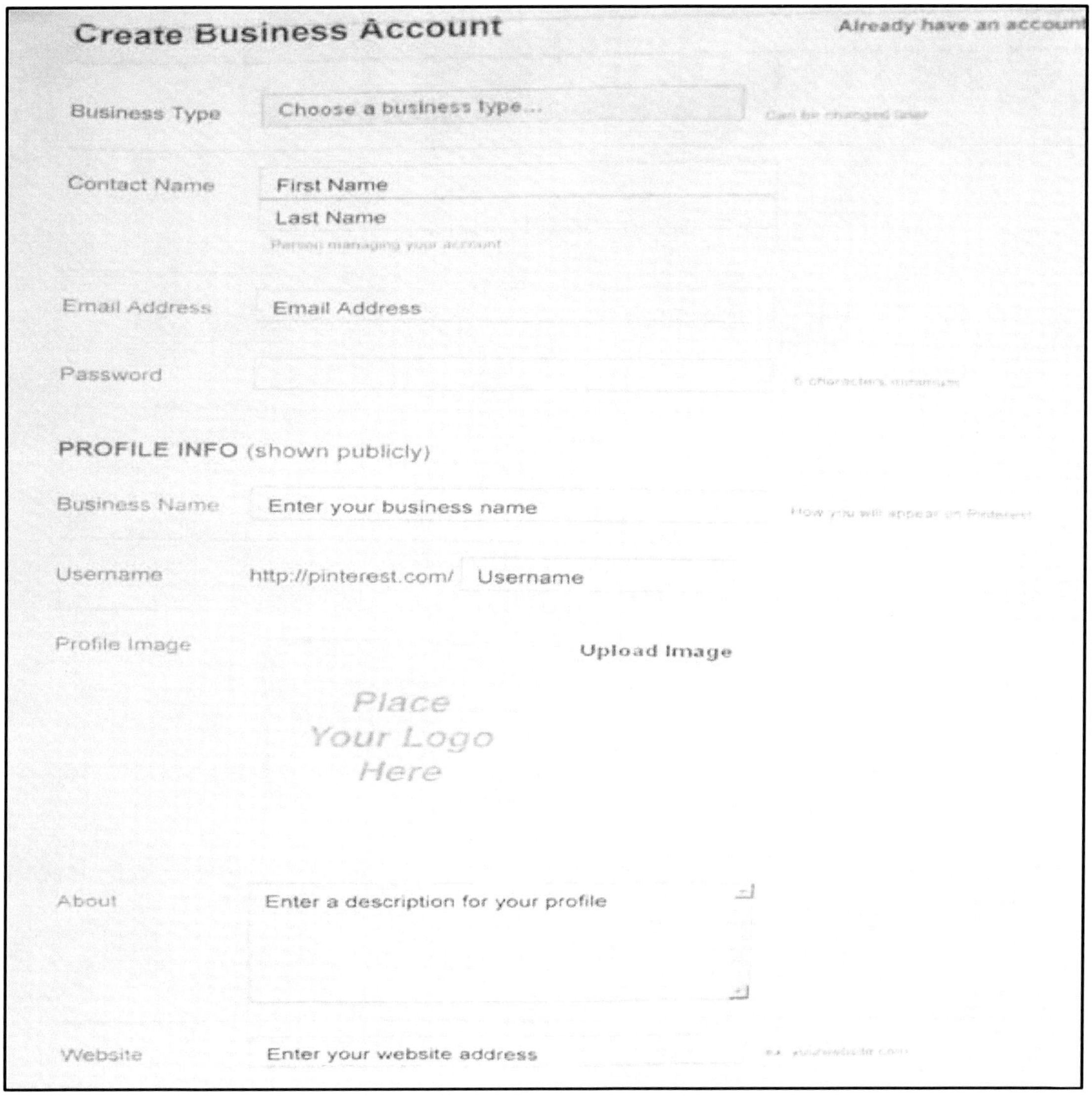

Figure 4 Data screen for creating a business account.

Once you have an account you can also adjust your email notification options in your "Settings," which will be listed in the dropdown box under your name at the top right corner of your Page (figure 5). You have the choice to control when/if Pinterest emails you every time someone likes, comments, repins your content, follows one of your boards, etc. An important note about your "Settings:" make sure the "Search Privacy" box is on <u>OFF</u>. Otherwise,

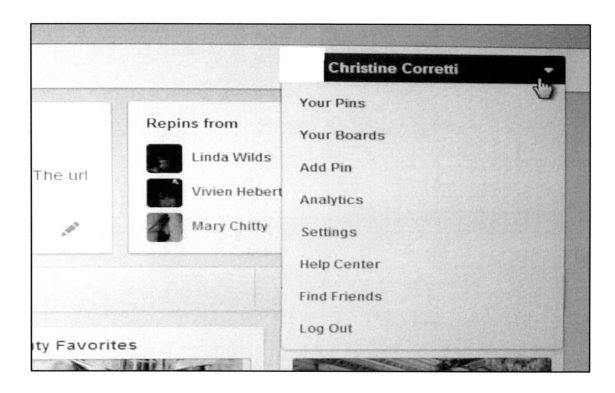

<u>Figure 5 Drop down box under one's name at the top right of one's Pinterest Page</u>.

Pinterest will prevent search engines from including your Page in search results.

Verification

The next step in setting up your Pinterest Business Page is verifying your website. Click on the tiny pencil at the right of your profile photo to edit your settings, where you'll be able to click on the phrase "Verify Website" to the right of your url. Three steps follow:

1. **Download the HTML verification file**.
2. Upload this file to your web server.
3. **Click here** to complete the process.

Click "**Download the HTML verification file**." A confirmation screen will say "Looking good! You are ready to return to the verification page and complete the process. Go to Pinterest."

1. Click "Go to Pinterest" and you will come back to **"Download the HTML verification file**." Select the latter. (Do <u>not</u> choose the option to use metatags.)

2. Save the downloaded file to your Downloads folder.

3. Next, login to the C-Panel (Control Panel) of your webhosting site. I shall use Blue Host as an example.

4. Click on Bluehost's Files, then on File Manager (figure 6).

5. Bluehost's File Manger Directory Selection box will show up. Click on Web Root (public_html/www) (see figure 6).

6. Next, choose the Upload command on your C-Panel site.

7. Click the html file in your computer's Downloads folder.

8. You will then be returned to Pinterest's verification

page. Click on the highlighted terms "**Click here** to complete the process."

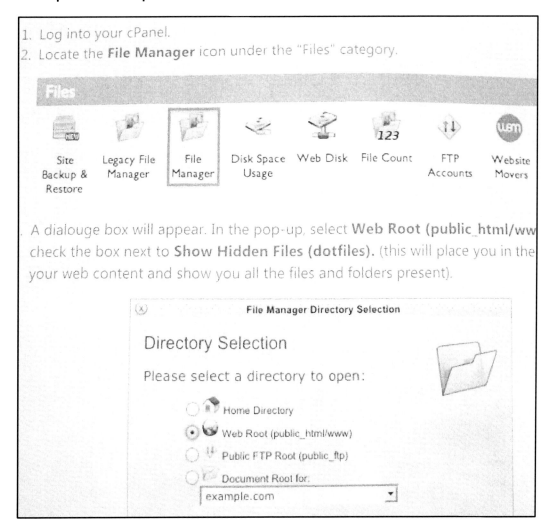

Figure 6 Bluehost's File Manager and File Manager Directory Selection.

Verification is complete. Your website url (which will lead the clicker to your actual site) will be at the right of your profile picture with a check mark beside it indicating you have approval to use Pinterest for commercial purposes. That is important because your status as a business will encourage viewers to think of themselves as your potential customers. Once your website is verified it will show up in Pinterest's server and therefore in online searches. If you do not verify, you will be left with a Profile Page, which will not appear in Pinterest related searches.

One note about Business Pages you should keep in mind is that, at this time, you cannot verify your business url if it is part of another company's website. For instance, Pinterest will not allow you to verify your Etsy shop's url because the latter is rooted in Etsy's main website.

Other differences between a Profile and a Business

Page are the business Terms of Service and the advantage of receiving notice from Pinterest of new ways to engage with and market your products to the Pinterest community. Current information on effective marketing practices is found on business.pinterest.com, which you should consult immediately.

Both business and personal Pinterest account holders have the option of adding the "Pin It" button, "Follow" button, "Profile" widget, or "Board" widget to their websites. Doing so will enable and encourage others to visit you on Pinterest and to pin material from your site onto their own Pinterest boards. From there your pins will attract new visitors to your website and Pinterest Page.

"Pin it" Button

Go to business.pinterest.com again. There, under a few case studies, you will see buttons and widgets available to pinners. To create the "Pin It" button (which is also listed under "Goodies" at the top of about.pinterest.com), first select if you'd like the pin count (the number of times an image was pinned from a website) above or beside your button. You can also choose to have no pin count at all. The next step is to opt for the button to appear near one image, or all of your images (note: if your website has no images you will not be able to use the "Pin it" button). If you decide upon the latter alternative you will have just one more step: Pinterest will formulate the "Pin it" button's code for you to copy and paste into your site HTML.

If you choose to have the "Pin it" button on just one image, type in the url for the image's page, the image url, and a caption to describe the image. Pinterest will then give you a code to copy and paste into the relevant space on your site HTML.

Also note that Pinterest plugins, such as Pretty Pinterest Pins, are available via website creation software (i.e. WordPress).

Remember, your url will automatically show under images that viewers pin from your site, so you need not worry about copyright issues. Nevertheless, if you'd like, you can feature a copyright notice to pinners on your Pinterest Page and/or your official business website.

"Follow" Button

The "Follow" button invites those who visit your website to your go to your Pinterest Page. Select "Follow," then enter your Pinterest user url. The code to copy and paste into your site HTML will be generated for you.

"Profile" Widget

The "Profile" widget enables you to display up to 30 of your latest pins on any part of your website. Simply add your Pinterest user url in the given box; then Pinterest will pick up your recent pins and provide you with a code to copy/paste into your website HTML. The "Profile" widget is valuable because new pins will diversify your website with no extra effort on your part. Plus, this widget makes it possible to showcase a variety of images all in one place, while still encouraging viewers to find more on your Pinterest Page.

"Board" Widget

The "Board" widget has the same value as the "Profile," but is more focused: as its name suggests, this widget allows you to show one of your Pinterest boards on your website. You will need to choose a particular board that fully stands for your business and add its url to the "Board" widget box. Pinterest will generate the code to copy and paste into whatever space you'd like the "Board" widget to appear.

Create and Curate

As previously stated, Pinterest offers unlimited potential for what you can do to build brand awareness and interest in your products. Essentializing the nature of your product is vital to marketing, and Pinterest lets you do that through a most powerful means – visual stimulation. It is imperative, therefore, to create boards that stand out among the millions and millions of images on Pinterest.

Give each of your boards a unique, expressive title, that is, a heading that imparts your creativity, knowledge and expertise as well as the value and nature of your products. For instance, if you are selling vitamins, why not categorize them alphabetically and title each board according to benefit (i.e. "Vitamin C: Nature's Antioxidant"; "Vitamin E for Soft Skin," etc.)? Don't forget to use keywords that appear on your website (remember SEO).

You must also select one of the categories listed on the board creation screen, for that will enable your board to show up in Pinterest search results and in the main menu under "Categories" and "Everything." If you do not select a category your board will be very hard to find in Pinterest searches.

Use relevant keywords in the board's description box. You could begin your words with hashtags (i.e. #Etsy), which facilitate discovery on Pinterest and enhance SEO. However, don't overdo it. If you write something convoluted like this: #Pinterest #works #for my #Etsy #shop, you will detract readers from your Page. Instead, add a hashtag only to the most important words, and make sure to capitalize those terms: Pinterest works for my #Etsy #Shop.

Having between 30-50 boards on your Business Page is ideal (the current average for top pinners is between 30-

200), for the value of your Pinterest Page is all about boards and their contents. If you have just a few boards your audience will think your product selection is insubstantial. You need many images, remember, to stand out in the ocean of Pinterest pins and compete with other business' visual marketing campaigns. Boards, like their titles, are important sign posts for attracting a specific type of audience (women, men, book lovers, etc.) that will love your products and <u>want</u> to buy them.

That is why board covers are *extremely* important. They show who you are. If they attract and hold viewers' attention covers have the potential to convert visitors to followers and to buyers. To set a board cover of your choice simply hover your cursor over the board so the words "Change Cover" show up. Click on those terms. Then, the computer will give you an option to click through the pins comprising that board before you decide upon which one to affix. You'll even have the option to align the picture with your cursor by dragging the pin up, down, right, left. Click "Save" once you have finished adjusting the image. The computer will then set the board's cover into place.

I like to change some of my board covers now and then to freshen my Business Page's overall look. This is a good way to show my latest pins and to keep customers interested. If you follow my example make sure your new board covers do not stray from your Business Page's original theme. It is also wise to add a new board or two from time to time for added variety and to showcase new products you produce.

There are more, sophisticated ways to make your Business Page visually appealing. Harmonize your boards' colors by juxtaposing similar hues across a row, and gradually transition from light to dark boards by adding

medium shades in between. Consider that my first row,

Glorious Gems

Fine Fashion

Beauty Favorites

Interior Decorations

Figure 7 The first row of my Pinterest Page.

which I've segmented in two parts for this study, mostly

comprises an array of champagne, pale pink, creams, beige, and gold (figure 7). Jewelry; fine fashion; beauty products; and architecture/interior design are the subjects presented.

The next row continues the previous thread, incorporating browns, beige, and peach/pink/rosy saturations: my art and literature blog, whose cover is likewise architectural; my drawing of King Big Bear, the main character of my fairy tale, *A Father's Wish: the Tale of King Big Bear the Fat* is the cover of the next board, "Children's and Young Adult Literature." Of course, pairing the king with

My Fairy Tale / Art Blog   **Children's & Young Adult Literature**

Continued on next page.

Corretti Designs: Fashion   **Greeting Cards, Corretti Designs**

Nature by Design, Christine Corretti

Figure 8 The second row of my Pinterest Page.

his blog makes sense. Then come fashion illustrations by Corretti Designs; my and Carolyn Corretti's artwork in the form of greeting cards; and my nature drawings (figure 8). The first <u>two</u> rows (which are the most important for grabbing viewers' attention) show viewers what I am about immediately – an artist and writer, one who interrelates the arts and finds inspiration in nature and the work of other designers (jewelers, architects, perfumers, and fashion designers).

The third row begins with "Custom Illustration by Corretti Designs" (figure 9). Together, the second and third rungs tell the viewer that Corretti designs are sold in a variety of forms (originals and copies) and through different venues: my Fine Art America website http://christine-corretti.artistwebsites.com/ and custom orders from me. The third row continues to incorporate subject matter related to interior design: "Ladies' Tea Party" and "Vintage Vanities" both include pins by other Pinteresters in addition to a few of my drawings. "Architecture and Interiors by Christine Corretti" has, as the title indicates, only my own work. Some

Custom Illustrations by Corretti Designs   Ladies' Tea Party!

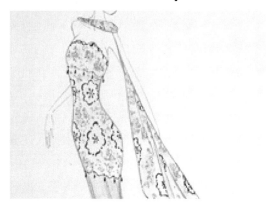 

Vintage Vanities   Architecture & Interiors by Christine Corretti

Children's Books

Figure 9 The third row of my Pinterest Page.

of the drawings in the latter board show up on my blog, so it made sense to end the row with "Children's Books." Here, I used *A Father's Wish* as a cover. King Big Bear sits in the middle of airborne roses that complement the floral designs on the previous rows. Notice that the boards in this section pick up the earthy, creams and pastel hues above them.

Rows four, five and six are, likewise, predominantly warm and pink/rosy. Their subjects are related to beauty, luxury and art, and most of them comprise work by other artists, photographers, and designers. I did, however, add a few of my perfume bottle drawings to the boards "Beauty: Image & Idea" and "Perfume Bottles." The board "Flowers" has a couple of my floral portraits. "My Etsy Shop" is the only board on this row with all items by me.

My Page gradually transitions to cooler and darker shades on the seventh row (figure 10). However, there are

Wedding Designs

French Beauty

Ocean Fruits: Pearls & Shells

Old World Jewelry

Fashion Illustration

Figure 10 The seventh row of my Pinterest Page.

still pastels to look at. Similar shapes and designs (i.e. flower bouquets) likewise smoothen the change. Most of the subsequent rows are even richer in tone: forest green, deep gold, black, are just a few; but I balanced the darker colors with cream, white, beige, pink and other pastels so rows on

Teddy Bears

Women in Art

Pale Designs

Doll Houses & Miniatures

Figure 11 Some boards from the lower half of my Page.

top would blend in naturally (figure 11).

Much of the bottom half of my Pinterest Page explores subjects and themes at top – for instance, "Fashion Illustration," "Old World Jewelry," "Animal Bliss," and there are new art forms to see here – "Doll House Miniatures" and "Exquisite Dec Arts." I also added additional boards (i.e. "The Midas Touch," "The Emerald City," "Pink, Peach, Mint, & Lavender Stones," and "Ocean Foam") that show how objects become more beautiful when color coordinated (figure 12).

Pink, Peach, Mint, & Lavender Stones   Ocean Foam

Figure 12 Color themed subject matter.

Literary boards for adults are featured toward the bottom: "Historical Fiction" and "Books on the Arts." Such educational material is vital to my pursuits, as it is to other artists, writers, and, generally, people who enjoy the humanities (figure 13).

Historical Fiction   **Books on the Arts**

Figure 13 Two of my book boards.

I must admit that the group boards on indie literature, and online business (i.e. "Pinterest Infographics") at the Page's base do not match those above them. But that is alright. I have no control over their layout because I didn't create these boards myself. The important thing is that they are there to help fellow artists, writers, and entrepreneurs.

As a whole my Business Page is feminine, sophisticated, ornate, richly colored, soft, fairy tale oriented, and solidly grounded in art, design, learning, career advancement, beauty, luxury, and nature.

My example shows that diversifying your Business Page so that it stands out in the Pinterest crowd involves exhibiting every facet of your professional expertise. You should try to tell a story, or make statements about how your different talents complement each other through a particular arrangement of your boards, as I have.

Experiment frequently with your board covers and board arrangement to find the best ways to enhance your Business Page's visual appeal. Adding a new board from time to time will help to add variety and new patterns to your

Page. To change your boards' arrangement just drag them with your mouse. The computer will save the new layout for you.

Once you have created your boards, make sure to add content (pins) to <u>all</u> of them as soon as possible. Leaving a board blank, or with just a few pins is unprofessional, boring, and will deter visitors from becoming followers. Whenever I create a new board I immediately add 25-35 pins to it.

Pin regularly (perhaps every two hours when you have a promotion, or product launch going on) so your followers will think of you often (remember, they will receive your pins in their image feed). Do not pin all at once and then never again, for consistency is key to keeping viewers' interest alive and attracting new followers. The best times of day to pin are Thursdays and Fridays after 5 p.m., when most people wind down from the work week; and the weekends, when people have the most time to shop online.

It is now mandatory to add a description (however short) on each pin (popular pins have one or more sentences to explain, educate, entertain, incite curiosity, attract attention, tell a story – even one that continues on your website; in fact, you might think of boards as miniature books that open up to a set of pins that tell a story in picture and/or verbal form). You could use hashtags before a few key words within the description. Do not forget to add your website address as well. Apart from telling viewers where to purchase your product, your pin's url is a backlink to your site that helps your webpage rise in Google searches. A hashtag at the start of your site's url may, however, deactivate the web link, since hashtags tend to activate only the words they touch. Click on the hashtagged url to make sure it does in fact lead to your website. You should also do the same for urls without hashtags.

A great way to really get your pin noticed is to put relevant business info (web url, company logo, blog post heading, etc.) on the image itself – without blocking/cluttering the picture, that is. If the product featured is for sale add the price in the pin's description. Pinterest will automatically affix the price to your image; that will encourage people to consider a purchase, and will make the item appear under the "Gifts" heading in Pinterest's menu box. Specifying who the item is for (i.e. children) in the pin's description is also a good way to maximize your product's potential to show up in topic-related searches on Pinterest.

Most people, including authors who have written on the subject, do not know that pins with affiliate links are risky. If your website showcases products from, say, Amazon, and you, as an Amazon Affiliate, receive a percentage of each item's cost when someone buys it through your website, naturally, you may want to attract customers by advertising your affiliate products on Pinterest. However, if you have hundreds of affiliate pins Pinterest will delete your Page. It is better to have fewer than 20 affiliate pins and a note in your board description that more (affiliate) items are for sale on your website.

All pins, whether they represent a business product or not, should be at least 80x80 pixels, but do not concern yourself so much with size, as Pinterest recently updated all pins by making them about 25% larger. Your pins should also be colorful and clear enough for someone to admire. Photograph the products you sell from different angles, at close range, and in natural light. Vertical pins are quite popular on Pinterest because they take up more space, but these should not be too long, since people will lose interest if they have to scroll far down to see the entire pin. Further, since the commands to pin and like are at the top of each image viewers will grow wary of scrolling back up to reach these buttons. Videos are becoming popular – in fact, there's now a videos option in the main menu box -- and so are clear, bright/pastel infographs, and other types of pins with writing on them. Literature, charts, and graphs diversify a "canvas" of pictures and, like images, can grab attention, stimulate questions and intellectual conversations. Rewrite your blog posts onto Pinterest to show your knowledge and expertise, and, if you can, add a tutorial on how to use your products. Tutorials have been quite successful on Pinterest because people want to know how to get the most out of what they will potentially buy.

Your pins should be original. They should tell the viewer about your "personality" as a writer, artist, designer, photographer, etc., and stand for the whole range of your product selection, and your talents, as suggested earlier. All the while they must appeal to your targeted audience's interests and desires. That is not to say, however, that you shouldn't intersperse a few pins from other brands/pinners throughout some of your boards. If you have a cosmetic company, and one of your boards focuses on lipsticks you produce, including a few lip colors from popular brands/boards/pinners (see the "Popular" heading in the menu box) will improve your rankings in Pinterest searches: i.e. if a pinner enters "Lancôme" in the Pinterest search box, your Lancôme pins and your name will come up. You can also do the reverse by weaving your products into a board on a broad array of brand names.

Another way to diversity your boards is to gather images from the web that have not been pinned, or are seldom pinned. Since not every website has "Pin it" buttons near its product images you can manually add the "Pin it" bookmarklet (essentially the "Pin it" button) to your computer's Bookmarks Bar, where it will be ready whenever you find an online item you'd like to add to your Pinterest Page. Get the "Pin it" bookmarklet at the following address: http://about.pinterest.com/goodies/.

Each type of browser (i.e. Chrome, Firefox, Safari) has a different way of enabling you to add the "Pin it" bookmarklet to your Bookmarks Bar. (Youtube offers tutorials on each method.) The following technique is the one I am familiar with: Google Chrome's.

1. Sign into your Google account.

2. Go to "Settings," then "import Favorites."

3. Under "Appearances" select "Always show the Bookmarks Bar."

4. Then visit http://about.pinterest.com/goodies/ and click the last two words (highlighted) in the question "Looking for the Pinterest Bookmarklet?"

5. Your computer will do the rest. You'll see the "Pin it" icon on your bookmarks tab.

Since a key component of the Pinterest experience involves discovering new things, displaying original pins in the most eye-catching ways will separate you from the crowd. Therefore, once you fill your boards with pins, you should apply the principles of style I have discussed in relation to board covers. Juxtapose complementary colors, shapes and sizes so your pins will stand out more beautifully against one another (figure 14). The order in which you pin images shows up on your boards in reverse; i.e. what you've pinned last shows up as the first image on your board. Coordinate your pins accordingly. Here's a tip: sometimes I gather

Figure 14 Four pins from my board "Glorious Gems".

images I know I'll add to a board by "liking" them. Then I

study how they look together in my "likes" file before I

arrange them in a similar way on my board. There is,

however, a possibility that Pinterest will listen to user feedback by enabling pinners to rearrange the order of their pins by dragging the images with their cursors.

Pinterest recently modified the state of a pin in its enlarged form. When a viewer clicks on a pin he/she sees a mini display of the contents of your pin's board at the right of the enlarged image. The viewer will also see a button that leads to the website from which the pin originated. More pinned items from the company in question are featured in the lower right hand corner, and at the bottom are other boards that have that same image, as well as similar items from other pinners (figure 15). The benefit of the previous configuration is obvious: both the mini board display and the additional items at the lower ends are meant to elicit the viewer's curiosity. The preceding should inspire you to pin your best and curate your images wisely.

Figure 15 Enlarged pin showing board origin at upper right.

Stylistic sensitivity improves over time, so be sure to study what other pinners (such as myself!) have done and aim to achieve like results. If you do, you will be most well prepared to attract and keep new followers, practices the next chapter will discuss in more detail.

Chapter 3 Traffic and Sales: Proven Ways to Build a Massive Following

The main point of having a Business Page on Pinterest is to advertise your products/brand to a targeted audience, as shown.   Millions of people using the site are your potential customers. They are there in good part to discover new things, new ideas, and new brands. But how, precisely, can you attract as many viewers with tools that are available on site? The "follow" system is the most common route to take. However, leveraging that method's dynamics for your business' success is not as self-explanatory as it may seem.

To follow a person on Pinterest simply click the "Follow" button near his/her name. (To unfollow that person click the same button again and it will turn back to the bold faced word "follow.") When a person follows you Pinterest will email you the notification.   If someone follows all your boards Pinterest will advise you to follow that person in return, for etiquette's sake. You are not, however, obliged to do so, but it is worth visiting your new follower's Pinterest Page to see if he/she has something of interest to you. If what you see is appealing, then you should follow that person back, for connecting with like-minded people is key to building a *faithful* following on Pinterest. For one, those who share your interests are more likely to purchase your products. If you are a designer of children's clothing, for example, you should follow individuals with children (you might see pictures of their sons and daughters on their boards); those who write for children; school teachers; day care workers, and the like.   I consider this type of follow a sincere one. It shows that your wish to connect stems from authentic care about who these people are, what they stand for, what they do. Further, your sincerity will increase your chances of their following you in return.

Other ways to show your interest is to comment on their pins. Less than 7% of time spent on Pinterest is used to comment; so those who do leave replies are more likely to be remembered. It is acceptable to ask for a follow in your comment, but make sure that what you've written is polite, not least because other pinners will see your statement. To comment, click on the pin to enlarge it. You will see a comment box below the image. Pinterest will email the person to whom you directed your comment that you've done so.

You can even tag your reader's name (like this: @Megan) so it will show up more easily on Pinterest. If you have insight (i.e. offer a solution to a problem; give advice), then the potential to bring all your readers to your side will be greater. That chance will also increase if the pin you comment on belongs to a board with many, many followers.

Further attract others by writing about what you do for a living, but don't seem like someone who is only looking for buyers.

Indeed, one of the biggest mistakes businesses make on Pinterest is coming across as insincere and even insensitive by pitching their products too aggressively. That is not a way to build trust, to endear and befriend your peers and potential consumers. You do not want to come across as someone who is on Pinterest just to make money. This type of aggression, combined with mismatched interests, will not bring you a good following.

Seeking out like-minded pinners should involve following those who follow your favorite pinners. Never forget, the likelihood that a person will follow you once you've followed him/her is high. Another tip is to connect with people who are following <u>fewer</u> pinners themselves; that way, your pins will be more readily seen in their image feeds because those feeds are smaller. Naturally, those who follow a great number of pinners get a load of images in their feeds and, therefore, have no time to look at all of them.

Conversely, you should follow those who have many followers, so when popular pinners repin your images your pictures will end up in more image feeds. From there your pins can go viral. This is an instance where you actually don't need many followers for your pins to meet a great number of people. For instance, if you have one follower with a few million followers one repin from her could have an enormous impact on you. Your pins can also travel onto many, many boards over time, even if you don't have many followers.

Software made for Pinterest, i.e. Pinbot and Ninja

Pinner, will save you time by following pinners for you. These robots usually gather hundreds of people within a few hours, and can run on auto-pilot all day and night. However, pin robots have several disadvantages. They will not cultivate relationships for you, largely because many of the pinners you will have amassed will not share much in common with your boards. Therefore, these people will likely not want to follow you in return. Indeed, you'll appear as an insincere follower: one who gathers pinners indiscriminately and only for profit.

Note that Pinbot gives the user an option to "repin after following." If you do that then random pins will enter your boards by the hundreds. Even if you do not "repin after following" foreign pins will infiltrate your "likes" file. Removing the latter necessitates manually "unliking" each of them.

A most highly effective way to gain followers is to repin and "like" others' images. Each time you "like," or repin someone's pin(s) Pinterest will notify that person via email that you've done so and even tell him/her the name of the board(s) you've pinned his/her material onto. That will inspire your potential follower to see what his/her pin(s) look like on your board(s), and perhaps to sift through your whole Page for images of interest to him/her. Your name and picture as well as the pin(s) you've "liked" or repined will appear to the left of his/her image feed, and in the (numbered) notifications drop down box at the upper right of one's Page, and therefore have the potential to attract a curious observer. Don't forget, repining others' images implies that you're willing to engage in relationships with them and are not on Pinterest just for your own personal gain.

Another tip is to get people to follow just one, or a few

of your boards if those are the only ones with images that match their interests. Indeed, pinners follow individual boards more than often than they do entire Pages. Here's why: a topic search usually organizes results according to board type.

The preceding ways to build a following on Pinterest will work best if you repeat them over time. Nothing happens overnight, and so you should include "follow time" in your daily Pinterest activity schedule.

Group Boards

A good way to connect with fellow Pinteresters and to increase your following and the visibility of your pins is to belong to one or more group boards, which are so designated by a "crowd" icon (figure 16). To invite others to pin to a group board you created yourself click on the word "Edit" at the board's base; then, in your board's settings enter one name at a time in the box designated "who can

Figure 16 The crowd icon appears here beneath the group board's title.

pin." Pinterest will send your invitation to the invited individual's email and Pinterest image feed. Once the person has accepted the invitation the group board will show up on the last row of his/her Page, and from there he/she will be able to edit the board – that is, leave the group if desired. In case your contributors forget who the board's creator is your name and profile picture will be shown at the top of the board's settings screen.

Group boards are practically necessary for businesses because they can get a lot of exposure. The key is to invite as many contributors as possible and to ask your followers to encourage their friends to join. For this reason, you should include your contact information in the board's description and/or specify that a request to join be made via a comment on one of your pins.

Group boards should be related to your interests and to those of your contributors, since those people and their followers will be potential customers and friends. Ideally, they should share their knowledge and expertise with you, other board contributors, and pinners who are not part of the group board. That way your group board will be considered most valuable to/by the Pinterest community and attract many followers. If what you have to offer is fun and personally beneficial group board members will readily add desirable content to your group boards and gladly repin your pins, which will, of course, end up in their followers' image feeds. That is why you should start a lasting conversation with your most productive contributors: comment on their pins, email them, and follow up more than once. But that doesn't mean you don't have the option to go to your Page's settings and choose to refrain from receiving email notification every time a person adds a pin to your group boards!

Naturally, group boards work well for affiliate marketers; so be sure to add your website url to your affiliate pins before they arrive on your group boards. You should specify to those whom you invite whether or not it is acceptable for them to sell products on the group board. If they do add a price tag to their pins that will make your group board a mini-mall and therefore attract many visitors who are willing to shop.

If you are invited to a group board, please read the creator's protocol. Some people who use Pinterest do not want contributors to sell things on their group boards, and will remove those who pin against the rules. If you yourself are a group board's creator and you'd like to remove a pinner simply visit the board's settings to do so. Note as well that if you delete another contributor's pin(s) (only a board's creator can do that) Pinterest will automatically remove that person from your group board.

"Pin it" Contests

An effective way to engage an audience and to find new followers while advertising your products is to have a "Pin It to Win It" contest on one of your boards that showcases your best products, preferably a group board you've started yourself. Pin the contest's instructions and your contact information at the top of your board, and include a picture of the item you will give away to the person who wins by, say, creating the most insightful theme-based board featuring some of your pins. Once the contest's deadline has passed and you have a winner, acknowledge that person on your "Pin It to Win It" board. That way, your followers will know you as someone who cares about the person behind the pinner. The following are some ways to run a successful "Pin it to Win it" contest:

1. Offer a products you usually sell as the free gift. Or, give away something that is related to your business in another capacity. For instance, if you sell pet grooming products your free gift could be a book about dog breeding. The gift should benefit your followers, make them happy, and inspire them to buy from you in the future.

2. Run your contest at a time of the year (seasonal or holiday) when shoppers spend a lot (i.e. Christmas). If this is a holiday contest you might even specify that your pins are gift ideas for different types of people. That will let your audience know how helpful you are as a Pinterest contact and as a business.

3. Tell your followers to hashtag and repin your pins onto boards that are theme-related; that way, your images will meet a welcoming audience; and the

hashtags will enable you to keep track of the pictures that are pinned for the contest when you enter your pins' titles in Pinterest's search box.

4. Ask your followers to repin onto their own group boards. Perhaps, as an incentive, give each group board pinner an added entry into the giveaway drawing.

5. Encourage your contestants to invite their friends to join your "Pin It to Win It."

6. Advertise your giveaway on Facebook, your blog, or any other social media site to which you belong. Ask your friends on those platforms to invite their friends to enter your Pinterest contest.

Pinterest recently put together a set of rules governing "Pin it" contests that you should keep in mind.

1. Do not specify, or imply that Pinterest endorses your contest.

2. Don't require people to pin solely from one selection of images.

3. No person is allowed to repin your contest rules.

4. Do not count a pin, repin, like, follow, or board as an entry into a sweepstakes.

5. Do not ask for comments.

6. No pinner is allowed to vote with a pin, like, repin, or board.

7. Keep the number of your "Pin it" contests reasonable. Don't overdo it.

But that is not to say you can't have a board for your past, present, and future giveaways, which should give viewers an added incentive to follow, or keep following you.

"Pin It to Win It" contests are highly effective for new

businesses that need more exposure and customers. These competitions are fun, and pinners who participate don't forget the people who run them. Remember, you need to build a loyal fan base in order to succeed on Pinterest and any other online platform. Just as your product selection has to be original, your presence on Pinterest must be dynamic enough to keep people interested in what you have to offer. A "Pin It to Win It" contest will add an extra surprise to your pot, a new way to excite followers and pique their curiosity about your business as a whole.

The next chapter will explore how businesses have excelled with/on Pinterest, but, while we are on the topic, let's look at how one company fared with a "Pin It to Win It" contest now. In 2012 HSN created a buzz about its home décor line by holding a "Pin to Win" contest for which each contestant created a board out of HSN product pins that stood for his/her idea of a dream room. The boards were tagged #HSN and #HouseBeautiful so they could become highly visible to the Pinterest community as a whole. The pinner with the best board won the HSN furnishings from her dream home board. The rationale behind this contest was to focus on a popular Pinterest category – home furnishings, "dream home" décor in particular --- as a way to tell pinners that HSN's home products are perfect for one's domestic ideals. The prize was generous and surely inspired others to look out for future HSN "Pin It" contests.

Secret Boards

Another good venue for group activity and promotional launches is the secret board -- in essence, a storage space for ideas, images, articles, books, etc. that a pinner wants to keep private. His/her reason for doing so may be to shield information from competing brands, or to plan a future event.

I've used secret boards to collect images I intended to organize at a later date, and I've also kept secret space for business articles I gathered on Pinterest and planned to read in the future. You might use a secret board for business collaborations, or other projects that involve pooling ideas and continuous revision.

To get started, go to the bottom of your Pinterest Page. Beneath your last row you will see a line of demarcation. Under that line are three blank templates (at this time Pinterest does not allow a user to have more than three secret boards) marked "Create a secret board." Click on the template to go to its settings screen. You will see that the "Secret" option is "On." Invite your colleagues by typing in their names, or email addresses in the "Invite" box, just as you would for group boards. Once you want the board to go public turn the "Secret" option "Off." Be careful about your decision, for once you've made a secret board public you cannot make it secret again.

The secret board is, then, another tool for a successful Pinterest marketing strategy, for with it you can enliven your content, keep it surprising, well organized, and have your customers anticipating more from you in the future.

<u>Measure your Results</u>

To gage how your following is sharing your pins go to
the drop down box beneath your name and select

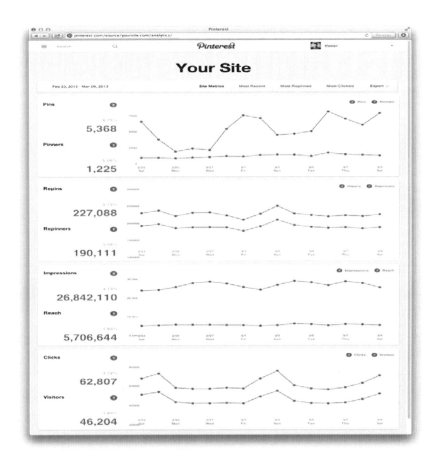

<u>Figure 17</u> <u>Pinterest's Analytics tool for Business Pages.</u>

"Analytics." This new tool, available only to those who have
verified websites/Business Pages, consists of several graphs

that track your pins' weekly progress (figure 17). The first graph shows the number of images pinned from your website and how many people pinned them. The second graph indicates the number of repins and repinners; while the third shows the number of times your pins appeared in Pinterest image feeds, on boards and Pinterest's main page, and in search results. Here, you will also see the number of people (or "reach") who saw these impressions. Graph four shows how many clicks to your website originated from Pinterest, as well as the number of people who visited your site from Pinterest.

At the top of your graphs are five headings: Site Metrics, Most Recent, Most Repinned, Most Clicked, and Export. The first four are more detailed breakdowns of data in your graphs. Click on "Export" to download your Analytics to your desktop. You can also access the number of pins from your website and of those who pinned them by going to http://pinterest.com/source/yourpinterestname.com/.

Studying your Analytics will enable you to figure out what you did right, or wrong during the time represented on your graphs. You could even keep a written, illustrated log by your computer to keep track of how you marketed your material on Pinterest each week. Repeat the methods that worked best and even combine them with new approaches. Just remember to consult your Pinterest analytics regularly, as successful businesses, next chapter's focus, do.

Chapter 4 How Businesses have Succeeded on Pinterest

Elite companies have managed to gather hundreds of thousands, even millions of followers on Pinterest. They have done so partly because they are already household names. However, it is clear that big businesses are also combining strategies discussed in this book to achieve success on Pinterest: they are visually dynamic, socially interactive, sensitive to consumers' needs and desires, informative, practical, and original.

Etsy

Let's consider Etsy an admirable example (figure 18). An online site with over 800,000 individual shops and over 15 million unique handmade and/or vintage items, Etsy channels into some of the most popular categories on Pinterest – crafts, jewelry, home goods, and clothing. The company has 65 boards, each well stocked with colorful, detailed images of unique things that epitomize Etsy's diversity. Together, the boards cover a variety of topics, and none show just one type of product. Each board concerns an occasion (i.e. weddings, Halloween), or function entertaining), or group of people (kids), décor/design, and

Figure 18 A segment of Etsy's Pinterest Page.

the like. Concomitantly, the company's Page displays a plethora of Etsy products that are suitable and beneficial for each subject. These boards are, in essence, tutorials – popular types of pins, recall, for they instruct by <u>showing</u> how their items may be used. The multi-faceted content of Etsy's Business Page indicates that the company has much to offer numberless aspects of our lives.

Etsy's Pinterest Page is, in sum, a place where we can shop, as well as get ideas from others – for the creativity of its contributors is what Etsy is all about. The presence of guest pinners on the company's Page stresses that fact. These people show that Etsy is a community of everyday people from all over the world (in addition to U.S. shops, there are foreign boards: "EtsyUK," for United Kingdom shops, "EtsyFr" for French Etsy products, etc.) and that viewers can find their own creative niches and open shops on www.etsy.com themselves. However, the guest pinners stand out from the crowd in one way: they all have over 100,000 followers on Pinterest. Perhaps they are guest pinners because of that fact, or maybe their presence on Etsy's Page led Pinteresters to their side. Either way, the guests are encouraged to repin Etsy material, and when they do these images will widen Etsy's audience tremendously.

Etsy has a Sweepstakes board, which is a fine way to attract customers and encourage people to repin images. But perhaps putting the sweepstakes board at the bottom of Etsy's Page is not the best idea; then again, Etsy already has a massive following, and the company's fans likely will make an effort to scroll down to the end and see the Sweepstakes sign.

Sephora

Like Etsy, Sephora realizes that the visual nature of

Pinterest is well suited to marketing wearable items. Since Sephora carries hundreds of cosmetic and fragrance brands, the company's Pinterest Page is highly varied, as it should be. No one board is dedicated to a single name. Instead, boards are organized according to the most popular topics in the beauty industry, on runways and magazines, and on women's minds, such as "Red Carpet Beauty"; "Trending Now"; "Pro Tips." And each board advertises more than one company's items --- all of which can be used to achieve the looks showcased on that particular board. The message is that Sephora has everything a woman needs to be on trend and look her best. Similarly, the multitude of written and video tutorials on Sephora's Pinterest Page assimilate techniques one can apply with a variety of items sold at Sephora.

Sephora's Business Page is an educational catalog that

links ideas with products so viewers can believe in the company's technical and aesthetic expertise.

Neiman Marcus

The Pinterest Business Page of Neiman Marcus is different because each of the company's boards has a title beginning with the words "The Art of." We see "The Art of Shoes," "The Art of Living," "The Art of Orange," and so on

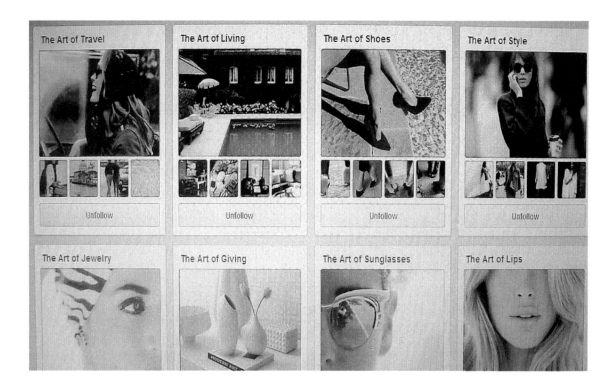

Figure 19 A section of Neiman Marcus' Pinterest Page.

(figure 19). Neiman's is a high end department store, and its Page suggests that its merchandise is what luxury living, a proverbial art form, is all about. Indeed, the company even has a board titled "The Art of Neiman Marcus." Neiman's boards are made up of pins that show you how to *combine* their products for a luxury lifestyle. Not surprisingly, a good number of these pins come from Neiman's catalogs, which showcase seasonal trends and how to wear them for different occasions.

The only thing that, in my opinion, detracts from the quality of Neiman's Pinterest Page is the disorganization of board topics. For instance, food and beverage boards appear at opposite sides of the Page, interspersed with some boards that have no relation to fine dining. In the previous respect, Neiman's Pinterest presence is a bit distracting. If the viewer is interested in a category and wants to learn more about it he/she has to scroll through the whole Page to do so, if he/she thinks of searching that far.

Chobani

The Pinterest Page of the yogurt brand Chobani is a must-see if you are using Pinterest for business. The first board, called "Go Real," ("Life's real, so are we" is the board's description) encapsulates what the brand is about --- *organic* yogurt --- and sets the tone for subsequent boards that focus on healthy eating; though the first board includes mottoes that define what being "real" is (i.e. "Be you, bravely") without alluding to food. But that is alright, since quotes are quite popular on Pinterest. Surely, Chobani is aware of that fact. The motto pins lend themselves to repinning onto many types of boards, which will lead new eyes to the Chobani name and Page.

Rows consist of different ways to use Chobani yogurt:

"Baked with Chobani," "Dip and Dish with Chobani," "Protein Parfaits and Smoothies," "Tastes Better with Yogurt." The message here is that Chobani yogurt is versatile enough to use in many dishes; therefore, you should buy it in great quantities. Further, using Chobani is a good way to add protein to any dish. As the description for the board "Protein Parfaits and Smoothies" mentions, Chobani has twice the amount of protein of other yogurts. That message appears on the smoothie and parfait board for another, more particular reason: athletic people drink protein shakes to build muscle.

Not all the pins making up Chobani's boards involve Chobani products. The company is smart to suggest that it cares more about its customers' well-being than about competing with other brands and businesses by excluding them from its Pinterest Page. (That message harks back to the saying on the first board, "Real friends get treated like family.") Chobani advertises foods from other names, as well as recipes from culinary blogs and websites, such as "Sweet Treats and More" www.sweettreatsmore.com/. The latter are important to Chobani, however, because they are venues where one can learn to use Chobani products.

The TomKat Studio

Kim Stoegbauer, freelance stylist for HGTV, DIY Network, Pottery Barn Kids, and founder of the TomKat Studio, a blog/website that offers a plethora of party ideas and craft supplies, has a Pinterest Page that assimilates every aspect of what she does. All of Kim's boards are packed with items they convey the endless variety of what you'll find on her site (figure 20). The top boards are some of the most important: "Pretty Things I Love," "Parties I Love," "TomKat Free Printables," "Shop TomKat," "Pottery

Barn Kids Projects," and "HGTV Projects." "Pretty Things I Love" introduces Kim's aesthetic, which lights up her Page as a whole: girly, feminine, pastel things that are party/craft-

Figure 20 A few boards at the top of TomKat Studio's Page.

related. The next board, "TomKat Free Printables" invites viewers to try her printable party PDFs (i.e. invitation patterns, cupcake holders, etc.). Those who receive her freebies will likely come over to the "Shop TomKat" board and from there visit, and purchase party PDFs on www.TheTomKatStudio.com.

Many of Kim's boards showcase different types of parties she designed and supplies that go along with them: "TomKat Parties for Girls," "Strawberry Party Ideas," "Lollipop Party Ideas," "Barbie and Paris Party Ideas," the list goes on. But even though many of the pinned items are sold on her website, Kim also features related products from other brands, such as Zulily, which has pretty clothes for little girls. In this way Kim demonstrates her talent as a stylist and her ability to work well with other companies. The same message informs Kim's boards for HGTV, DIY Network, and Pottery Barn Kids.

Other Professionals who can Benefit from Pinterest

Interior Designer

Show your expertise in decorating homes by creating boards whose pins are the prettiest rooms in your clients' homes. Photograph them in natural light and from different angles and ranges so viewers can appreciate textures, color combinations, spatial organization, and the like. You might have the top boards for styles you usually work with and bottom boards for aesthetics you seldom do. Each board should have your or your company's name. If you work as part of team, then boards showcasing collaborative projects is essential. You might even make the latter group boards to which your colleagues contribute (so far, I have not seen this type of group board on Pinterest; hint: originality counts).

Photographer

Create one or more boards for each type of photo you take and fill them with your best shots. If you work at weddings be sure to create at least one board for your wedding photography, as Pinterest is a popular site for planning nuptial events. You can further attract brides-to-be by including a board on wedding dresses, another on honeymoon spots and fine hotels, one on wedding cakes, etc. Intersperse your own photography pins throughout these other boards. It is also a good idea to have pins that show what types of cameras you use – i.e. top quality ones, as well as how-to books on photography, which can be useful to online marketers.

Fitness Professional

Fitness boards are becoming more popular on Pinterest. Usually, boards about exercise include video tutorials and infographs on weight loss rates, but what you don't see as much is scientific information about metabolism, causes of specific types of weight gain, and other medical news. If you are a fitness expert including pins with such data will set you apart from the crowd and further enhance your credibility. Of course, a fitness professional should be learned in such matters anyway.

Emulate the Best and Offer Something More

The preceding should help you choose which business practices to adapt and apply to your Pinterest Page. There are, arguably, endless ways to reach others on Pinterest, some of which will bring more results than others. But the important thing is to test numerous methods of attracting eyes, driving traffic to your website, and building a loyal fan base of customers. The key to earning trust is to have personal relationships with your customers. Remember, Pinterest is a *social* media site. Consumers and clients will return to you if you use Pinterest to reach out to them as people and engage with them in a friendly manner. For instance, you could offer them advice; ask if they're enjoying what they bought from you; and encourage them to sign up for a newsletter that teaches readers how to get the most out of your products. You might even befriend some of your clients through Pinterest and keep the relationship going through other social media sites, like Facebook, which the next chapter will discuss.

Chapter 5   Spread Your Pinfluence Further by Linking Pinterest to other Social Media Sites

Facebook

The effort to expand your following on Pinterest should include linking your Pinterest Page to other social media venues you enjoy. You will find that many using the latter are also looking for new Pinterest followers. (More than 9 million pinners have connected their Pinterest accounts to Facebook. Take advantage of that!)

As I mentioned earlier, you may sign up for a Pinterest account with your Facebook login data. After you've done so go to your "Settings." Scroll to the bottom of the page and make sure the Facebook on/off button is "On." If you've never signed in with your Facebook data before you can do so now by going to your "Settings." You can also link to Facebook by clicking on the respective icon to the right of your profile photo and left of the editing pencil. Once you've linked Pinterest to Facebook your new pins will appear on your FB Page. If you want more options, including the ability to have all your boards visible on Facebook, install the Pinterest app or tab (developed by the company Woobox) for Facebook at http://apps.facebook.com/pinterestpagetab/ The FB sign in screen will come up before the computer leads you through a few simple steps. Note, you should have your Pinterest Page address, which is designed in the following way: http://pinterest.com/yourname/, handy for this process. The Pinterest tab (a red letter P) will appear just beneath your FB header image. When someone clicks on that tab all your boards will show up on a screen linked to your FB Page. And from there your pins will be available to the clicker!

It is likely that viewers will click on your Pinterest tab because it will have a prominent position on your FB Page.

Plus, the large red letter P stands out naturally. But if you'd like to further stimulate sharing you can add a message about the Pinterest tab on your timeline and/or ask close friends to tell *their* friends to check out your boards.

Conversely, you can pin images from Facebook to Pinterest by implementing this little known method:

1. Install the "Pin it" bookmarklet to the top of your browser, as instructed earlier.

2. Right click on the Facebook image you'd like to pin and select "open image in new tab."

3. Now click the "Pin it" bookmarklet and you will be able to pin the FB image.

Twitter

The Twitter icon is also to the right of your profile picture, and the same steps for linking Pinterest to Twitter follow on and through your Pinterest "Settings" menu. Tweet and retweet your best pins regularly, especially during a promotional period.

Email

Another way to link online platforms is to click "Invite Friends" in the dropdown box under your name. You will then get four options: email, gmail, Yahoo!, and Facebook. The last three will work only if you've already used their respective login data to create a Pinterest account; but the "email" option is open to everyone. Just fill the given boxes with the email addresses of friends you'd like to invite to Pinterest. If you have an email subscription form on your website/blog you could send an invitation to all those who've signed on; but just emphasize that joining you on Pinterest is purely optional.

If you are connected to the preceding venues you will be able to take advantage of the "Share" button at the top of an enlarged pin (figure 21). That button streamlines the process of sharing individual pins, not boards.

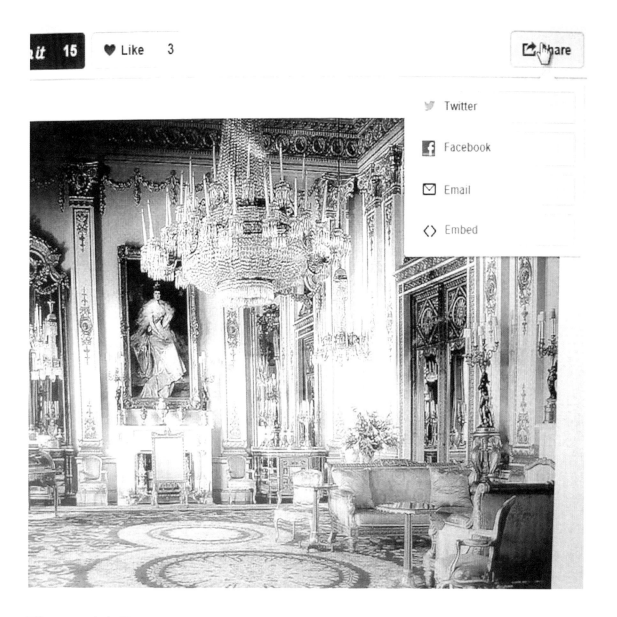

Figure 21 Enlarged pin showing sharing buttons.

Your Pinterest Page in Cyberspace

Whatever social media site you connect to your Pinterest Page should give your followers there a reason to join you on Pinterest. Consider these options:

1. Mention that your Pinterest Page has a wider selection of products than your Facebook Page, LinkedIn Profile, etc. do.

2. Stress the aesthetic appeal of your pins. Regularly post one or more images from a favorite board onto your FB timeline, Instagram platform, etc., and include a detailed description of what the respective board has to offer. Don't forget to add your Pinterest url in your message.

3. Tell readers/viewers there's a promotion, or offer that is up and running on your Pinterest Page and nowhere else.

4. If you're a writer tell a story on, say, Facebook, but don't give the ending on that platform. Instruct your peers to come to your Pinterest Page at a later date, when you will reveal the story's conclusion. For those who are not authors: apply the same "seek and find" strategy for an upcoming event, launch, etc. on Pinterest.

After testing what works best for your business, repeat your favorite methods of engagement over and again. Keep to a few social media platforms so you can give each of them due time. Just remember to promote campaigns across multiple channels as you see fit.

One reason why you should do the preceding is that more and more businesses are connecting their Pinterest Pages to other social media sites. Big businesses are especially involved in showing off their pins on Facebook through the Woobox tab I discussed earlier, and through Tabfusion's Pinterest app for Facebook. On the other hand, small businesses are those who use Pinvolve, an app that allows specific pins, not boards, to appear on Facebook.

Be on the lookout as additional Pinterest software is made for a variety of social media platforms. Some of those tools will be redundant, but others, no doubt, will help you keep up with your competitors.

Chapter 6 Pinterest's Oncoming Impact on Internet Business

A further indication of Pinterest's increasing influence throughout the digital world is the inclusion of a Pinterest app in Barnes and Noble's Nook tablet. Pinterest itself offers an app for e-readers and another for mobile phones/cameras. (Go to http://about.pinterest.com/goodies/ to access these features.) Clearly, there's a belief that the opportunity to discover and learn on Pinterest enriches the reading experience. And that is something authors should take advantage of: join Pinterest and upload your book covers, blog posts, story snippets, giveaways, book signing events, and more. Word and image go hand in hand in the digital world, and both should be shared together.

But perhaps the visual aspect of the online world will become more important than ever because of Pinterest's influence. It is possible that in the future the blog will lose some of its value. So, to prepare for such developments make sure to embellish your written content with a lot of visual material. In addition, your website/blog should have as many sharing buttons (the "Pin it" button, the Google+ button, and the Facebook button, etc.) as possible so your material can be visible to the widest audience.

The tools Pinterest has given us to disseminate our content and to measure shares suggest that Pinterest wants businesses to succeed. It is therefore likely that Pinterest will offer paid advertising on its site; that would only make sense, given the number of those who use the platform. Paid ads would, furthermore, make Pinterest more enticing to entrepreneurs who have yet to join.

Conclusion

In light of the preceding discussion it is hard to believe that Pinterest is currently in its beta phase. But the platform's growth rate suggests that in the near future Pinterest's following will be explosive. So now is the time to establish your Page and curate your best content, which will maximize your potential to attract existing and newcoming pinners. Just as crucial to your success is your ability to cultivate a faithful client base. When someone follows you on Pinterest take the time to find what that person is about. If he/she matches your interests then follow that person back and consider befriending him/her. That is the way to be authentic, sincere.

Networking with other businesses on Pinterest is, likewise, most important. There is nothing wrong with creating group boards for others in your niche, or asking someone for an invitation to his/her group board. Just make sure to offer something in return when a fellow entrepreneur does you a favor. Keep the relationship with your peers going on other social media platforms too.

You should even advance your business by familiarizing yourself with upcoming tools, insights and other insider information on business.pinterest.com. Pinterest will doubtlessly come out with news ways to expand your reach on its site and from there on other social media platforms.

If you implement the practices put forth in this book you will build a memorable presence on cyberspace and a business that <u>lasts</u> as long as there's a digital world to enjoy.

About the Author

Christine Corretti, Ph.D. is an art historian, artist, and author who enjoys all things beautiful and bookish. Visit her literary/fairytale/art blog/website *Chronicles of King Big Bear* http://www.chroniclesofkingbigbear.com/ and her Fine Art America site http://christine-corretti.artistwebsites.com/

She would love to connect with you on Pinterest--- http://pinterest.com/chcorretti/

CPSIA information can be obtained
at www.ICGtesting.com
Printed in the USA
LVXC02n1630081213
364351LV00013BA/174